Ongoing Personal Evangelism

Ongoing Personal Evangelism

Factors That Influence Evangelism

John P. Davis

Foreword by Mitch Glaser

RESOURCE *Publications* • Eugene, Oregon

ONGOING PERSONAL EVANGELISM
Factors That Influence Evangelism

Copyright © 2021 John P. Davis. All rights reserved. Except for brief quotations in critical publications or reviews, no part of this book may be reproduced in any manner without prior written permission from the publisher. Write: Permissions, Wipf and Stock Publishers, 199 W. 8th Ave., Suite 3, Eugene, OR 97401.

Resource Publications
An Imprint of Wipf and Stock Publishers
199 W. 8th Ave., Suite 3
Eugene, OR 97401

www.wipfandstock.com

PAPERBACK ISBN: 978-1-6667-1074-8
HARDCOVER ISBN: 978-1-6667-1075-5
EBOOK ISBN: 978-1-6667-1076-2

07/23/21

Unless otherwise indicated, all Scripture quotations are taken from the Holy Bible, Translation New International Version®, NIV®. Copyright © 1973, 1978, 1984, 2011 by Biblica, Inc.™ Used by permission of Zondervan. All rights reserved worldwide. www.zondervan.comThe "NIV" and "New International Version" are trademarks registered in the United States Patent and Trademark Office by Biblica, Inc.™

Dedication

IN JUNE OF 1951, I was born into the home of Jim and Bert Davis. In 1970, Jim Davis personally led me to a saving knowledge of Jesus Christ. Before going to college, for the next year and a half, I was my dad's visitation partner and saw firsthand how to share the gospel. Of course, I had grown up with a dad who never met a stranger and who was always ready to speak of the free salvation in Jesus Christ.

In 1972, I was introduced to Dr. Bill Schroeder, who was then pastor of Oak Forest Baptist Temple in the Chicago suburbs. Not only did I end up marrying his daughter three years later, but I had the amazing experience of seeing someone practice ongoing personal evangelism. Dad Schroeder was another soul winner who was at ease in talking to strangers about Jesus.

Both of these men impacted my life with their love for the gospel, their joy in the gospel, and their courage in sharing the gospel with others.

Contents

Dedication | v
Foreword by Mitch Glaser | ix
Introduction | xi

1. Biblical-Theological Foundations for OPE | 1
2. Factors That Influence OPE | 20
3. Research Undergirding the Eight Factors | 33
4. Implications of the Eight Factors | 40

Appendix A: Evangelism Questionnaire | 53
Appendix B: Ongoing Personal Evangelism: Training Outline | 56
Bibliography | 59

Foreword

I HAVE BEEN ASKED by my friend Dr. John Davis to write a foreword to this excellent book about evangelism—an essential and joyful duty for all who love the Messiah Jesus and believe him to be their Savior and Lord. The title does say it all, as I am sure you will find *Ongoing Personal Evangelism* to be an inspirational tool that will help you and those you shepherd share the gospel with intentionality, with social and cultural sensitivity to those who do not know him.

On a personal note, I can say that after reading this book, I am more knowledgeable and eager to make personal evangelism a more important part of my life. I hope you will have this same experience! I made the eternity-transforming decision to follow Jesus fifty years ago, coming from a Jewish home and a secular lifestyle. I have served as a missionary to my own people most of my life and a good amount of that time in my hometown, New York City. Brooklyn, where I live, is incredibly diverse, filled with almost every nationality under the sun. The world has come to Brooklyn, where John Davis and I became fast friends and served the Lord together for a number of years.

I can tell you from personal experience that John has the experience to write this book. He is a committed disciple of the Lord Jesus and has spent his life sharing the message of Christ to individuals, crossing cultures and languages, driven by his love for the Lord and desire to fulfill the biblical mandate to make disciples.

Foreword

This is an important book for many reasons, but perhaps the most significant is that it presents a fresh approach to personal and church-based evangelism. The research is excellent, but in a book like this, the researcher himself is even more critical to the exchange of information. Dr. Davis is an accomplished personal evangelist and pastor. He is a classic reflective practitioner who enacts what he writes. This is why the book would be an excellent tool for all who are deeply interested in communicating the message of the gospel to those who are not yet believers.

John is used to speaking to bright, dedicated Christians, as well as to immigrants from African and Latino countries. Dr. Davis speaks to and trains Christians regularly, and this is evident from his easy-to-grasp writing style and ability to connect with everyday Christians. He does so intelligently, with solid biblical and sociological information. Dr. Davis is a wonderful distiller of God's truth and has the ability to synthesize information across disciplines, which is critical when you are training people for outreach. To be effective on this topic, one needs to understand both the Bible and people.

He is able to both teach and communicate insightful biblical truths and practical lessons learned from a lifetime of presenting the gospel in everyday life.

Dr. Davis expresses his intended goal and impact the book will have on those who read it:

"The hope and prayer of this author is that every believer will accept the privilege and responsibility of personal evangelism and that this book may encourage an understanding and a pursuit of these contributing factors in their lives."

Ongoing Personal Evangelism is biblical, practical, concise and powerful! I hope it inspires you and deepens your love for the Lord and the lost, as it did for me.

Dr. Mitch Glaser

Introduction

SINCE BECOMING A FOLLOWER of Christ in 1970, I have pursued what I call *ongoing personal evangelism* (OPE). I define OPE as the regular, personal, and intentional practice of interacting with non-believers, and verbally sharing the gospel of Jesus Christ with the intent to call for a commitment. OPE includes planting, watering, cultivating, and reaping.[1]

For me, each word of the above definition is important. *Regular* implies that evangelism is habitual, not sporadic. *Personal* distinguishes this evangelism from other types, such as crusade evangelism, church event evangelism, visitation evangelism, open-air evangelism, tract distribution, etc. Personal also refers to one's individual participation in sharing the gospel of Jesus Christ with those who are lost. *Intentional* indicates that there is an underlying commitment and a purposeful involvement in evangelism. *Practice* assumes that evangelism is more than a theory to be discussed but is something to be applied. *Interacting with non-believers* presupposes the necessity of having occasions to actually do evangelism. *Sharing the gospel of Jesus Christ with the intent to call for a commitment* postulates that the gospel is a verbal communication about the death and resurrection of Jesus Christ for sinners (1 Cor 15:3–4) that seeks a response of repentance and faith. Ronald W. Johnson sets forth clearly that sharing the gospel is the heart of evangelism:

---

1. Petersen, *Evangelism as Lifestyle*, 25.

Introduction

> Evangelism is the process by which the good news is shared. While there are many definitions of evangelism and many methods, and while evangelism means many things to many people, the bottom line must be always evaluated by the faithfulness of the witness in sharing the gospel with the lost around as to the best of our ability and as a result of our Lord's command.[2]

In my forty-five years of pastoral ministry I have observed that only relatively few Christians maintain a regular practice of OPE. Though having trained many in numerous and various evangelism programs over the years, the conclusion was yet the same: relatively few Christians maintain involvement in OPE.

At the same time, I faced the conundrum that many who are considered to be mature Christians do not practice OPE. Maynard-Reid expresses a similar concern for the low priority that evangelism has had in evangelical Christianity.

> We are faced by a bleak reality in North American Christianity, even in evangelical Christianity: we are turned off by evangelism. Among most Christians, evangelism has therefore taken a backseat and become a low-priority agenda item, and some even make straightforward objections to it.[3]

Though this general lack of evangelistic activity was evident, at the same time it was apparent that some Christians still practice OPE. In most evangelical churches and parachurch ministries, there are at least a handful of people who maintain a passion for and practice of reaching lost people. Through a Doctor of Ministry project, I set out to discover common factors in the lives of Christians who practice OPE.

Identifying those factors benefits the church of Jesus Christ. Perhaps many of those factors would be teachable and trainable.

In this book I will discuss those factors that exist in the lives of those who practice OPE, some of the research behind those factors, and some of the implications for evangelism. However, before

2. Johnson, *How Will They Hear*, 5.
3. Maynard-Reid, *Complete Evangelism*, 135.

we look at those factors, it is important to lay a biblical-theological foundation for the responsibility of OPE.

1

Biblical-Theological Foundations for OPE

DONALD A. MCGAVRAN CONCLUDES from the New Testament that any believer who is spiritually healthy is involved in evangelism.

> No one can be *fully* biblically sound and spiritually renewed without being tremendously concerned about the multitudes of unreached men and women and, indeed, of unreached segments of society.[1]

If McGavran's statement is true, then a biblical-theological survey of evangelism should set forth clearly the responsibility of personal evangelism.

The biblical responsibility for all believers to be involved in personal evangelism and the accompanying factors can be supported in a number of ways:

1. The portrait of God in the Old Testament, which presents him as One who seeks the lost

2. The example of Christ, whom all believers are called to follow (Matt 4:19)

---

1. McGavran, *Effective Evangelism*, 37.

3. The example of the disciples, who are the foundation of the church
4. Christ's commissioning of the church
5. The example of the early church, which went everywhere preaching the word of God (Acts 8; 1 Thess 1)
6. The frequent admonitions of New Testament epistles
7. The example of Paul
8. The nature of the gospel message as a verbal communication

The following survey discusses the relationship of each of the above to OPE.

The Old Testament Portrait of God

Concerning the presence of personal evangelism in the Bible, John Stott remarks: "Ever since Jesus spoke to the Samaritan woman at the well of Sychar and Philip sat beside the Ethiopian in his chariot, personal evangelism has had impeccable biblical precedent."[2] Actually, personal evangelism has even deeper roots that go back to the Old Testament.

The first act of personal evangelism is found in Gen 3, when God seeks to bring Adam out of hiding. God asks, "Where are you?" The Hebrew word is translated by three English words. It is an interrogative pronoun with a second person masculine singular suffix. God designs a personal question that causes Adam to personally evaluate what is presently happening in his life in relationship to God. God himself models the first activity of personal evangelism. He speaks words that expose Adam to his guilt.

From this point on, the Old Testament furnishes numerous examples of God's seeking the lost and calling individuals to himself. It is clear that God's concern is to redeem some for his own glory. Willem VanGemeren summarizes this Old Testament concern with redemption:

---

2. Stott, "Christian Ministry," 244.

Biblical-Theological Foundations for OPE

The history of redemption unfolds a progression in the outworking of God's plan of redemption that will unfold completely in the restoration of all things. All blessings, promises, covenants, and kingdom expressions are reflections or shadows of the great salvation in Jesus Christ that is to come at the end of the age.[3]

The call of Abraham in Gen 12 issues forth a whole new focus in God's plan of redemption. This text focuses on the personal call of an individual, one who is then called to mediate God's blessing to others. The following exegesis may serve to understand the significance of this text for personal evangelism.

Gen 12:1–3 introduces God's purposes with Abraham as a promise. The first four prefix conjugation forms in verses 2 and 3 are all cohortatives,[4] denoting God's resolve:[5] "I will make you into a great nation"; "I will bless you"; "I will make your name great"; "I will bless those who bless you." The one non-perfective, "I shall curse the one who treats you lightly," signifies a contingent future.[6]

The *vav* preceding the cohortative signifies either purpose or result after the imperative *go*.[7] Yarchin adequately defends the command/promise structure of Gen 12:1–3.[8]

The combined sense is that God says to Abraham, "Go . . . to the land I will show you that I may make you into a great nation, that I may bless you, that I may make your name great.'" The imperative with *vav* conjunctive signifies that these divine resolves have the further purpose that Abraham be a blessing. The first person cohortative and non-perfective of 12:3, "I will bless, I will curse," give the purpose/result of Abraham's becoming a blessing to others.

God filled Abraham with life that he in turn might mediate life to others, i.e., be a redemptive blessing to them. As Abraham

---

3. VanGemeren, *Progress of Redemption*, 26.
4. Waltke and O'Connor, *Introduction to Biblical Hebrew*, 565.
5. Waltke and O'Connor, *Introduction to Biblical Hebrew*, 580.
6. Waltke and O'Connor, *Introduction to Biblical Hebrew*, 511.
7. Waltke and O'Connor, *Introduction to Biblical Hebrew*, 577–78.
8. Yarchin, "Imperative and Promise," 164–78.

became a blessing, verse 2 ("be a blessing") describes how God fulfilled his purpose of bringing blessing to others. Here we have God initiating blessing for Abraham so that he can mediate blessing to others. Abraham's mediation of blessing to others was predicated on his authentic experience of God's blessing.

A conclusion drawn from these words to Abraham is that God intended for Abraham and his descendants to mediate the blessings of redemption to the world. This is an Old Testament parallel for speaking about personal evangelism, for ultimately the blessing of Abraham is tied to the gospel of Christ (Gal 3). This somewhat parallels the Great Commission, where the church is told to "go and make disciples of all nations." It then follows in the Old Testament that those who are called into relationship with God engage in the activity of calling sinners to reconciliation with God.

Ps 67 reflects on a national level the personal responsibility given to Abraham to be a blessing. As a result of God's blessing on his people, he intends that his people mediate that blessing to the world. Listen to the psalm:

> God be merciful to us and bless us,
> And cause His face to shine upon us.
> That Your way may be known on earth,
> Your salvation among all nations.
> Let the peoples praise You, O God;
> Let all the peoples praise You.
> Oh, let the nations be glad and sing for joy!
> For You shall judge the people righteously,
> And govern the nations on earth. Selah
> Let the peoples praise You, O God;
> Let all the peoples praise You.
> Then the earth shall yield her increase;
> God, our own God, shall bless us.
> God shall bless us,
> And all the ends of the earth shall fear Him.

This psalm speaks of more than just God's intent to have the nations praise him; it establishes the relationship between God's blessing his people and God's receiving praise from the nations of the earth. It is an important relationship, because understanding

Biblical-Theological Foundations for OPE

it may prevent God's people from seeking blessing selfishly and thereby prevent the church from becoming ingrown. We can infer from the psalm that spiritual authenticity produces worldwide proclamation.

The author of the psalm emphatically places a focus on the nations of the world by the use of three words translated either as peoples or nations. *Goyim* (used 1x in v. 2) describes all of those who were not Israelites—all non-Jews. Here in verses 3–5, *amim* (used 5x) and *leamim* (used 2x) are synonyms referring to ethnic communities, what we call people groups today—people who have unity because they share a relationship on the basis of common characteristics, such as language and culture. All of the words are plural and should be translated as such. The word in verse two is the word *goyim*, which means the gentiles. A gentile was anyone who was not a Jew. The other two words are synonyms, being translated as nations and peoples. Again, all words are in the plural and have the sense of ethnic communities. Not only does the psalm express God's universal intent for the earth's inhabitants, but it also expresses that intent geographically—"the earth, all the ends of the earth." The proclamation of the message is intended to cross all cultural barriers.

This psalm clearly sets forth God's desire that all the nations on planet Earth should praise him. The Jewish community of the Old Testament, which was God's missionary nation, spoke this psalm. Today, the sentiments of the psalm belong to the New Testament church, which God has ordained to spread the good news of his salvation to all the peoples of the earth. The psalmist's desire for grace, blessing, and favor is connected to God's desire that the peoples of the world come to know him. The psalmist had an unprejudiced desire for God to be showered with multiethnic praise.

King David reflects this evangelistic fervor in some of his psalms. He understood that one's personal experience of redemption should lead to sharing that experience with others. Listen to his words:

> He lifted me out of the slimy pit, out of the mud and mire; he set my feet on a rock and gave me a firm place to

stand. He put a new song in my mouth, a hymn of praise to our God. Many will see and fear and put their trust in the LORD. (Ps 40:2–3)

David provides another example in Ps 51:12–13, which reflects a personal evangelism motif: "Restore to me the joy of your salvation and grant me a willing spirit, to sustain me. Then I will teach transgressors your ways, and sinners will turn back to you." David understands that his experience of the gospel places upon him the responsibility to tell others.

Once again, it is clear that whether you listen to the prophets, poets, wisdom writers, or historians in the Old Testament, you find a God who is long-suffering, merciful, and full of compassion and who seeks lost humanity to be reconciled to him.

Though we may not be able to establish from the Old Testament that all of God's people were involved in OPE, we can conclude that God is an evangelistic God; that the Abrahamic covenant sets forth God's plan of redemption for the world; and that at least some individuals, like David, were involved in telling others about God's redeeming grace. We can see in the lives of those like David and Abraham that there was an authentic experience of God's grace and a corollary sense of responsibility to tell others.

The Example of Jesus Christ

Throughout the gospels, Jesus frequently encountered individuals evangelistically. Whether talking to the woman at the well, a demon-possessed man, a blind man, or someone like Zacchaeus, the tax collector, Jesus knew his mission:

> Jesus said to him, "Today salvation has come to this house, because this man, too, is a son of Abraham. For the Son of Man came to seek and to save what was lost." (Luke 19:9–10)

Jesus understood that the purpose of his life and death was to redeem sinners. His death "was not a mere martyrdom, but the vocation of the Servant through whose suffering and service the

Biblical-Theological Foundations for OPE

reign of God would be decisively established."[9] Consequently, he busied himself serving others, to the end that they might participate in redemption.

In Jesus's encounter with the Samaritan woman at the well (John 4), he modeled for us a degree of cultural sensitivity in a situation that required confronting many cultural taboos. He also demonstrated the importance of verbal communication in exposing individuals to their sin and need of the Messiah. Furthermore, he demonstrated the ability to start with felt needs and move to spiritual issues.

The commissioning of the seventy aptly expressed the compassion of Jesus for the lost and his sense of obedience in mission. A. B. Bruce describes the motive for this mission:

> Jesus still felt deep compassion for the perishing multitude, and hoping against hope, made a new attempt to save the lost sheep. He would have all men called at least to the fellowship of the kingdom, even though few should be chosen to it.[10]

Though Jesus often addressed the multitudes, he highlighted the importance of the individual. This is seen clearly in Jesus's trilogy on the lost coin, the lost sheep, and the lost son. The telling of these parables was in response to the well-grounded accusation that Jesus "welcomes sinners and eats with them" (Luke 15:2). Jesus told three parables to affirm their accusation and to show why he welcomes sinners and eats with them. Luke 15:10 encapsulates the message of these parables: "In the same way, I tell you, there is rejoicing in the presence of the angels of God over one sinner who repents."

Both Jesus's ministry practice and his teaching show the importance of working with individuals for a redemptive purpose and provide examples of cultural sensitivity, theological commitment, verbal communication, and spiritual authenticity in personal evangelism.

---

9. Wells, *Person of Christ*, 41.
10. Bruce, *Training of the Twelve*, 105.

Ongoing Personal Evangelism

The Example of the Disciples

Jesus's mission to "to seek and to save the lost" was an integral part of the call to discipleship. He said to those who would be his disciples, "Come, follow me, and I will make you fishers of men" (Matt 4:19). Ernest Best notes the importance of this call, saying, "The beginning of discipleship was the call and the commitment to fish for men."[11] The authenticity of the disciples' following Christ would be seen in their involvement in evangelism. Bill Hull also comments on the essential role of personal evangelism in the call to discipleship:

> There is no danger that Jesus would allow his followers to perish for lack of meaning. When Jesus calls a person, he calls him to a purpose, a dream, a goal, a life-changing vision. The vision is to be a fisher of men.[12]

The Old Testament provides the background for this fishing metaphor (Jer 16:16; Eze 29:4; Amos 4:2). The prophets portrayed God as a fisherman. However, fishing for men was an activity of bringing them into judgment. Jesus uses the fishing metaphor but reverses the intent. Jesus's disciples go fishing for men in order to rescue them from judgment.

The disciples' role as a community of responsible witnesses is highlighted throughout the gospels and is confirmed by Jesus' commission after his resurrection. A. J. Kostenberger notes the significance of the witness theme by Luke:

> Possibly invoking Isaianic "new exodus" theology, Luke notes that salvation will be proclaimed in Jesus' name to all the nations beginning in Jerusalem (Luke 24: 47; cf. Isa 43: 9–10). By the power of the Holy Spirit promised by the Father, the disciples' witness concerning repentance and forgiveness of sins in Jesus will extend to all nations, as the sequel to Luke's Gospel goes on to narrate (Luke 24: 46–49; cf. Acts 1: 8).[13]

11. Best, *Disciples and Discipleship*, 15.
12. Hull, *Jesus Christ, Disciplemaker*, 71.
13. Kostenberger, "Witness," 1002.

Biblical-Theological Foundations for OPE

The final words of Jesus recorded by Luke in his Gospel bring attention to the disciples' role as faithful and obedient witnesses to a specific event and message:

> Then he opened their minds so they could understand the Scriptures. He told them, "This is what is written: The Christ will suffer and rise from the dead on the third day, and repentance and forgiveness of sins will be preached in his name to all nations, beginning at Jerusalem. You are witnesses of these things." (Luke 24:45-48)

The disciples were a community of witnesses who were to be obedient to their mission. They were a band of men of different personalities (Peter and John) and representatives of various socioeconomic strata (Matthew and James). The mission superseded any personal differences or human inhibitions. The worldwide nature of the gospel and its theology was clear to them. Their authenticity as Christ's followers would be demonstrated in their becoming fishers of men.

The Great Commission

In the New Testament, the key text encouraging evangelism is Matt 28:18-20, commonly called the Great Commission:

> Then Jesus came to them and said, "All authority in heaven and on earth has been given to me. Therefore go and make disciples of all nations, baptizing them in the name of the Father and of the Son and of the Holy Spirit, and teaching them to obey everything I have commanded you. And surely I am with you always, to the very end of the age."

In Matt 28, Jesus stands on resurrection ground as the new covenant King. As the new covenant King, he commissions his followers with a task for the coming age. Because he is the new covenant King, his words must be taken seriously. Paul understood the kingship of Jesus in Ephesians. Listen to these solemn and powerful words:

> I pray also that the eyes of your heart may be enlightened in order that you may know the hope to which he has called you, the riches of his glorious inheritance in the saints, and his incomparably great power for us who believe. That power is like the working of his mighty strength, which he exerted in Christ when he raised him from the dead and seated him at his right hand in the heavenly realms, far above all rule and authority, power and dominion, and every title that can be given, not only in the present age but also in the one to come. And God placed all things under his feet and appointed him to be head over everything for the church, which is his body, the fullness of him who fills everything in every way. (Eph 1:18–23)

Again, Paul in Colossians describes the kingship of Jesus Christ:

> For he has rescued us from the dominion of darkness and brought us into the kingdom of the Son he loves, in whom we have redemption, the forgiveness of sins. He is the image of the invisible God, the firstborn over all creation. For by him all things were created: things in heaven and on earth, visible and invisible, whether thrones or powers or rulers or authorities; all things were created by him and for him. He is before all things, and in him all things hold together. And he is the head of the body, the church; he is the beginning and the firstborn from among the dead, so that in everything he might have the supremacy. For God was pleased to have all his fullness dwell in him, and through him to reconcile to himself all things, whether things on earth or things in heaven, by making peace through his blood, shed on the cross. (Col 1:13–20)

There is no question in the minds of the New Testament writers concerning the kingship of Jesus Christ. When he gathered with his disciples on the mountaintop, he spoke to them as a King and outlined for his subjects their task for the coming age until he would return again. What is this task? Very simply, it is calling people to follow Jesus Christ as Savior and Lord. The

Biblical-Theological Foundations for OPE

mission of the New Testament is driven by a call to obedience to the Great Commission.

The apostles understood this task and refused to be silent, even in a political and cultural climate that was antagonistic against the gospel. Apparently, they believed so much in the authority of the King that they were willing to suffer and even face martyrdom for obedience to the gospel task they were given. They did not even see their death as an obstacle to the advance of the gospel.

Since Jesus is sovereign over every square inch of planet earth, he has the legitimate authority to command his people to encounter every people group of the world and proclaim Jesus Christ as the only Savior and Lord. Christians are not to westernize but to gospelize every people group in the world. They proclaim to all people the exclusive message of salvation through faith in Christ alone: "Salvation is found in no one else, for there is no other name under heaven given to men by which we must be saved" (Acts 4:12).

The one imperatival phrase of Matt 28:19–20 is "make disciples of all nations." The other three verbal forms are participles that are subordinate to the main command. The first participle (go) is an aorist and is attendant to the main imperative, so that it takes on an imperatival sense: go. The other two participles (baptizing and teaching) are present active and adverbial, in that they define and accompany the main imperative. The Son of Man commands his church to be involved in the practice of OPE. Evangelism is a responsibility.

The Example of the Early Church

Jesus told his church to anticipate the gift of the Holy Spirit, who would empower them to witness about him. John Stott comments in regard to this mission:

> They would receive power so that between the Spirit's coming and the Son's coming again, they were to be his witnesses in ever-widening circles. In fact the whole interim period between Pentecost and the Parousia

Ongoing Personal Evangelism

(however long or short) is to be filled with the worldwide mission of the church in the power of the Spirit.[14]

The call to witness would be empowered by an authentic work of the Spirit of God in believers.

In Acts 8, Luke records the persecution that forced the church to move beyond Jerusalem in its mission. He writes in 8:4, "Those who had been scattered preached the word wherever they went." It is important to note that those who had been scattered were not the apostles. This demonstrates that the church in general understood that the responsibility for witness went beyond the apostles to each and every believer.

In Acts 8, Luke expands the importance of evangelism by accenting two different words: preach and evangelize. Both words entail verbal proclamation. John Stott notes the relevance of Luke's usage of these words for evangelism:

> A notable feature of this chapter is the currency it gives to two distinctively Christian words for evangelism. Luke has already described the apostles as bearing witness to Christ, announcing (*katangellein*, 4:2) their message, devoting themselves to the ministry of the word of God, and teaching the people. But now he introduces the verb *kerysso* ("to herald") in relation to Philip's proclamation of Christ (5), and popularizes the verb *euangelizo* ("to bring good news"). The latter he has used once before (5:42), but in this chapter it occurs five times. Twice the object of the verb is the towns or villages evangelized (25, 40), while the other three times the object is the message itself, namely the good news of "the word" (4), of "the kingdom of God and the name of Jesus Christ" (12), and simply of "Jesus" (35). This is a salutary reminder that there can be no evangelism without an evangel, and that Christian evangelism presupposes the good news of Jesus Christ.[15]

---

14. Stott, *Spirit*, 44.
15. Stott, *Spirit*, 144.

Biblical-Theological Foundations for OPE

Luke's record in Acts 8 of the evangelistic activity of the early church is foundational to our understanding of our responsibility for personal evangelism. D. S. Lim accurately asserts that the primary agents for evangelism in the New Testament were ordinary believers:

> The prime agents in evangelism were the ordinary believers (Acts 8:4; 11:19-21]), called "informal missionaries" (Harnack; Green). Wherever they lived or migrated, the good news spread by word of mouth through their natural relationships of families, friends, and acquaintances (cf. 1 Pet 3:15). As they "gossiped the gospel" with conviction and enthusiasm, people were converted and added to the church and its evangelistic force.[16]

The Admonitions of New Testament Epistles

The New Testament epistles disclose in many places the witnessing function of believers. For instance, the simile of Christians as lights is a witnessing simile, highlighting their need to live authentically and to be obedient:

> Do everything without complaining or arguing, so that you may become blameless and pure, children of God without fault in a crooked and depraved generation, in which you shine like stars in the universe, as you hold out the word of life—in order that I may boast on the day of Christ that I did not run or labor for nothing. (Phil 2:14-16)

Paul urges believers to walk wisely, speak graciously, be adaptable to changing situations, and pay the price to take advantage of evangelistic opportunities:

> Be wise in the way you act toward outsiders; make the most of every opportunity. Let your conversation be always full of grace, seasoned with salt, so that you may know how to answer everyone. (Col 4:4-5)

---

16. Lim, "Evangelism in the Early Church," 355.

Ongoing Personal Evangelism

Paul sets forth the church of Thessalonica as a model of spiritual authenticity and evangelistic activity:

> And so you became a model to all the believers in Macedonia and Achaia. The Lord's message rang out from you not only in Macedonia and Achaia—your faith in God has become known everywhere. (1 Thess 1:7–8)

Furthermore, Peter addresses the need for Christians to recognize their holy calling and be prepared to give a reasoned account of the hope they have in Jesus Christ:

> But you are a chosen people, a royal priesthood, a holy nation, a people belonging to God, that you may declare the praises of him who called you out of darkness into his wonderful light. (1 Pet 2:9)

> But in your hearts set apart Christ as Lord. Always be prepared to give an answer to everyone who asks you to give the reason for the hope that you have. But do this with gentleness and respect. (1 Pet 3:15)

All believers are not called to missionary activity like Paul's. However, all believers are called to bear faithful witness to the gospel of grace. William J. Larkin Jr. in his biblical-theological survey of evangelism notes that evangelism is for every member of the body of Christ:

> As modeled in the early church Paul teaches that the proper messengers of the good news are not only apostles and evangelists (Rom 1:9; cf. 1 Cor 9:18; Eph 3:5) and full-time Christian workers (1 Cor 9:14, 18; 2 Cor 11:7), but all the church of Christ (Eph 3:10; cf. Col 1:7). Every member must have feet shod "with the readiness that comes from the gospel of peace" (Eph 6:15).[17]

---

17. Larkin, "Evangelize, Evangelism."

The Example of Paul as a Pattern for All Believers

On numerous occasions, Paul called believers to follow his example. He saw God's work of grace in his life, as a pattern of God's work in other lives. Though Paul's unique role as an apostle precludes our seeking to follow him in every aspect of his life and ministry, the following verses indicate that imitating him in the work of the gospel was intended.

1 Corinthians 4:16 ("Therefore I urge you to imitate me") is in the context (vv. 11–13) where Paul details the tribulations he has faced for the sake of the gospel.

1 Corinthians 11:1 ("Follow my example, as I follow the example of Christ") is in the context of how Paul has lived with sensitivity to cultural diversity "so that they may be saved" (1 Cor 10:33).

Philippians 3:17 ("Join with others in following my example, brothers, and take note of those who live according to the pattern we gave you") is in a context where believers are called to model Paul's ethical behavior.

1 Timothy 1:16 ("But for that very reason I was shown mercy so that in me, the worst of sinners, Christ Jesus might display his unlimited patience as an example for those who would believe on him and receive eternal life") is in a context where Paul sets himself as a clear example of God's plan to mercifully save sinners.

In the preceding verses, the apostle Paul uses at least three different words that highlight his importance as a model for all believers—a pattern, one who is like another, and a standard. These words in their particular contexts stress the normalcy of Paul's practice of Christianity. Paul's life as a Christian is paradigmatic for all believers in many ways. At least three of these contexts, there is a gospel/evangelistic orientation. Paul is a model for personal evangelism. Listen to the self-description of his activity for the gospel:

> We proclaim him, admonishing and teaching everyone with all wisdom, so that we may present everyone perfect in Christ. To this end I labor, struggling with all his energy, which so powerfully works in me. (Col 1:28–29)

Another way we see Paul's model of commitment to evangelism is that he often requested prayer for his faithfulness in evangelism. His prayer requests reflected his desire to be a bold, clear, and obedient witness. He desired open doors through which the gospel could enter and spread rapidly:

> Pray also for me, that whenever I open my mouth, words may be given me so that I will fearlessly make known the mystery of the gospel, for which I am an ambassador in chains. Pray that I may declare it fearlessly, as I should. (Eph 6:19–20)

> And pray for us, too, that God may open a door for our message, so that we may proclaim the mystery of Christ, for which I am in chains. Pray that I may proclaim it clearly, as I should. (Col 4:3–4)

> Finally, brothers, pray for us that the message of the Lord may spread rapidly and be honored, just as it was with you. (2 Thess 3:1)

W. P. Bowers notes that Paul's public preaching and solicitation of converts was not unique in the Greco-Roman world of his day. However, what was particular about Paul's work was that he founded and nurtured believing communities. Clearly, accomplishing that necessitated personal evangelism. Bowers says, "Paul did indeed engage in missionary preaching stage by stage in his journeys. And he actively sought individual conversions as part of his calling."[18]

The Gospel as a Verbal Proclamation

The earliest usage of the verb *euangelizo* shows clearly that evangelism is a verbal proclamation. Consider the following texts from Luke:

---

18. Bowers, *Mission*, 936.

> The angel answered, "I am Gabriel. I stand in the presence of God, and I have been sent to speak to you and to tell you this good news." (Luke 1:19)

> But the angel said to them, "Do not be afraid. I bring you good news of great joy that will be for all the people." (Luke 2:10)

> The Spirit of the Lord is on me, because he has anointed me to preach good news to the poor. He has sent me to proclaim freedom for the prisoners and recovery of sight for the blind, to release the oppressed. (Luke 4:18)

In those texts of the New Testament that set forth a definition of the gospel, we see clearly that the *euangelizo* (the good news) is a verbal proclamation. Consider the following two texts:

> Now, brothers, I want to remind you of the gospel I preached to you, which you received and on which you have taken your stand. By this gospel you are saved, if you hold firmly to the word I preached to you. Otherwise, you have believed in vain. For what I received I passed on to you as of first importance: that Christ died for our sins according to the Scriptures, that he was buried, that he was raised on the third day according to the Scriptures, and that he appeared to Peter, and then to the Twelve. (1 Cor 15:1–5)

> But what does it say? "The word is near you; it is in your mouth and in your heart," that is, the word of faith we are proclaiming: That if you confess with your mouth, "Jesus is Lord," and believe in your heart that God raised him from the dead, you will be saved. For it is with your heart that you believe and are justified, and it is with your mouth that you confess and are saved. (Rom 10:8–10)

In the 1 Corinthians passage, the gospel is referred to as "the word preached to you." In the Romans passages, the gospel is "the word of faith which we are preaching." Both texts refer to the gospel as a verbal message that is spoken using either the word *logos*

Ongoing Personal Evangelism

or *rhema*, accompanied by the two verbs that have an active aspect (*euangelizo* and *kerysso*). Kittel firmly establishes that *logos* is the spoken word:

> The Word as Spoken Word. In all this the *logos* is always genuine *legein*, or spoken word in all concreteness. One of the most serious errors of which one could be guilty would be to make *logos tou Qeou* a concept or abstraction. Proclamation of the Christ event speaks the Word of God to the world. It is in the last resort a very sober fact, always taken into account by the men of the NT, that the Word is present to be transmitted. No one knows the Word without proclamation.[19]

Also, the word *rhema* equally implies a word that is spoken or uttered, i.e. "that which is said, word, saying, expression."[20] These words that define evangelism as verbal proclamation are consistent with those that are commonly used to designate evangelism in the New Testament. Lim notes the significance of the three Greek word-groups for evangelism in relation to verbal proclamation:

> Three Greek word-groups were commonly used to denote evangelism: *euangelizo* ("to share good news"), *kerysso* ("to preach"), and *martyreo* ("to bear witness:"). In reference to the act and/or process of telling others about Jesus Christ, the first is used most frequently in its verbal form accompanied by a word or phrase that describes the content of the good news, such as "the kingdom of God" (Acts 8:12) or "Jesus" (Acts 11:20), hence emphasizing the message's content. The second highlights the method of proclamation, as it originally denoted what a *keryx* ("herald") did. The third emphasizes the veracity and credibility of both the message and the messenger, for it was a legal term that referred to the attestation to facts and events based on the personal experience of the testifier.[21]

---

19. Kittel, "legw."
20. Arndt and Gingrich, *Greek-English Lexicon*, 742.
21. Lim, "Evangelism in the Early Church," 353.

Biblical-Theological Foundations for OPE

Evangelism then is the verbal communication of the death and resurrection of Jesus Christ in behalf of sinners, calling them to faith and repentance. In a modern world, where the means of verbal communication have multiplied, this would include the use of all audio, visual, electronic and literary aids for verbal proclamation.

More could be said about the responsibility of personal evangelism as being implied in the gift of the Spirit who himself is a witness to Christ (John 15:26), in the fact that believers are left in the world to witness (John 17:11, 18), and in the power of the gospel to transform us into witnesses (Rom 1:14-16).

Summary

This brief survey of personal evangelism leads to the conclusion that OPE is the responsibility of anyone who confesses Jesus Christ as Savior and Lord.

2

Factors That Influence OPE

IN VARYING DEGREES, THE foregoing biblical-theological study surfaces some of the factors that influence OPE. The prominence of spiritual authenticity, the verbal proclamation of the gospel, and the need for theological commitment is evident. To a lesser degree, we see the importance of community and cultural sensitivity. Though formal training is not discussed directly, the entire process of discipleship implies a training aspect. The significance of a particular personality type for evangelism is difficult to support. The emphasis in the Bible is on obedience and responsibility in evangelism, as opposed to giftedness.

We will now look at eight of the primary factors that surfaced from combining the biblical-theological study with readings from both literature on evangelism and my personal observations.

Factor One—Defining Evangelism

The first factor is the definition of evangelism. Do those who practice OPE define evangelism as a verbal sharing of the gospel, or do they accede to some broader definitions such as in David Barrett's "'Evangelize!' means 'Evangelize in 180 dimensions!'"?[1]

1. D. Barrett, *Evangelize*, 79.

My experience indicates that when a definition of evangelism is expanded to include such things as social work, the verbal proclamation of the gospel is often diminished. One reason for this is that many people who hold an expanded definition of evangelism view the good things they do to serve other as evangelism.

The writings of David B. Barrett demonstrate clearly that evangelism has been an ongoing concern and practice of the church since the death and resurrection of Jesus Christ till now.

A vast literature on the general subject of evangelism exists. Barrett notes that "titles strictly on 'evangelize,' 'evangelism,' or 'evangelization,' total 400 new books and articles every year; on broader definition, titles on evangelization and synonyms total 10,000 a year."[2] For the most part, this literature is on the popular level. The abundance of literature shows that the church has been concerned about this subject.

The definition of evangelism has become so broad, however, that the concept of OPE is nearly lost in the labyrinth. David Barrett, in tracing the history of evangelism, notes that the concept of evangelism has radically changed from "the strictly limited meanings that we have termed The Big Six—Preach! Bring! Tell! Proclaim! Announce! Declare!" to the current state of affairs where "'Evangelize!' means 'Evangelize in 180 dimensions!'"[3] Earl D. Radmacher expressed this same concern about changing definitions of evangelism over fifty years ago:

> Not only has the societal rebirth motif conditioned the motive of evangelism, but also it has infected the very heart of the message of evangelism. We find men actually telling us today that evangelism is not the saving of individuals but of the social, political, economic and cultural structures of life. One advocate defines evangelism this way: "Evangelism is social legislation."[4]

This reductionist mistake in defining the entire work of the church as evangelism is noted by Robert Coleman, as cited by

2. D. Barrett, *Evangelize*, 75.
3. D. Barrett, *Evangelize*, 79.
4. Radmacher, "Contemporary Evangelism Potpourri," 48.

Ongoing Personal Evangelism

Darius Salter: "Many Churchmen have such an all-inclusive view of discipleship that the specific work of rescuing perishing souls from hell scarcely receives attention."[5]

This author would concur with D. S. Lim's definition of evangelism that views evangelism as a verbal proclamation. In his excellent article "Evangelism in the Early Church," Lim writes: "Evangelism is defined here in the narrow sense of the verbal proclamation of the good news of salvation with a view of leading people to a right relationship with God through faith in Jesus Christ."[6]

Factor Two—Transformed Personality

Does the influence of one's personality and psychological makeup affect his involvement in OPE? Is there a particular personality type that is involved in OPE? Is personality a factor at all?

My experience with those who practice OPE indicates that more assertive and gregarious personality types are definitely involved in OPE. Yet, it is also evident that a sizeable percentage of others involved in evangelism are quiet and more introverted. The biblical data does not support a particular personality type.

Nevertheless, the literature suggests that personality is a consideration in the lives of those who practice OPE. Years ago William James in his classic work, *The Varieties of Religious Experience*, summarized key psychological factors in the lives of those who were deeply religious. In his own words, he summarized his findings with three beliefs and two psychological characteristics, as follows:

> Summing up in the broadest possible way the characteristics of the religious life, as we have found them, it includes the following beliefs:
>
> 1. That the visible world is part of a more spiritual universe from which it draws its chief significance;
> 2. That union or harmonious relation with that higher universe is our chief end;

---

5. Coleman, as cited in Salter, *American Evangelism*, 29.
6. Lim, "Evangelism in the Early Church," 353.

3. That prayer or inner communion with the spirit thereof—be that spirit "God" or "law"—is a process wherein work is really done, and spiritual energy flows in and produces effects, psychological or material, within the phenomenal world.

Religion also includes the following psychological characteristics:

1. A new zest which adds itself like a gift to life, and takes the form either of lyrical enchantment or of appeal to earnestness and heroism.
2. An assurance of safety and a temper of peace, and, in relation to others, a preponderance of loving affection.[7]

As James points out, one's psychological and religious experiences are intertwined. It is clear that the apostle Paul was self-aware of his personality but did not allow any perceived deficiencies of personality to impede his ongoing proclamation of the gospel.

> To be believable when one speaks is a wonderful gift that embraces many facets of personality, and all pastors cherish the ability to be recognized as those who speak with authority. For various reasons, some individuals are immediately perceived to be imposing, and for them the matter of credibility is less of a problem than for people of lesser gifts of presence or personality.
>
> Paul had this difficulty of credibility, and he attacked it in various ways (e.g. 2 Cor 11:21–30; 12:1–11 [2 Cor 12]). Perhaps the very Christian name he bore, "Paulos" ("Little"), indicated that this gifted servant of Christ felt some deficiencies of personality and was resolved to become known as the "little one" in the service of the Lord.
>
> Whether this is true, it is clear Paul expended much time and effort in making a credible case among Jews and Gentiles alike for the claims of Jesus Christ, an example all servants of the Lord should emulate.[8]

---

7. James, *Varieties of Religious Experience*, 377.
8. Harrison, "Pastor's Use of Old Testament," 130.

Casual observance and interaction with those who practice OPE suggests a preliminary conclusion that this practice goes beyond personality type. Common factors are the absence of fear and the presence of peace, both of which are the work of the Spirit common to all believers. Darius Salter emphasizes the importance of these two qualities: "Absence of fear and peace of mind are prerequisites to meaningful achievement in this life. Both can only come from knowing God and are requisites for the communicators who would preach the love of Christ."[9]

Factor Three—Spiritual Authenticity

One's spiritual development and pursuit of discipleship affects in some measure one's OPE. Most books on personal evangelism note the connection between authentic Christianity and faithful witnessing. Following Christ as Lord and living an authentic Christian life seem to accompany the practice of OPE. McGavran notes the relationship between spirituality and the practice of OPE:

> But biblical soundness and spiritual renewal will result in speaking to modern men and women around us in ways suited to their situation. Full biblical soundness and spiritual renewal will never permit Christians to make no effort whatever to communicate their faith and say comfortably, "that is the business of the pastor and Billy Graham."[10]

Also, Mittleberg and Hybels recognize the crucial role that spiritual development has in strengthening one's witness for Christ:

> When it comes to developing and maintaining high potency, there's no magic wand and there are no shortcuts. Our savor factor will be roughly proportionate to the extent to which we engage in the age-old spiritual disciplines.[11]

---

9. Salter, *American Evangelism*, 132.
10. McGavran, *Effective Evangelism*, 38–39.
11. Hybels and Mittleberg, *Becoming a Contagious Christian*, 44.

While Mittleberg and Hybels do not ever explain what these spiritual disciplines are, Douglas Rumford in his fine work *Soul Shaping* provides a helpful summary of spiritual disciplines. He recommends the following:[12]

Exercises That Increase Our Awareness of God's Presence

Repentance
Confession
Preview
Review
Prayer
Worship

Exercises That Help Us See Life with an Eternal Perspective

Bible study
Meditation
Spiritual reading

Exercises That Free Us from Evil's Power and Connect Us to God's Resources

Fasting
Silence
Solitude
Battling temptation
Prayer for spiritual battle

Exercises That Direct Our Lives toward Kingdom Purposes

Building character
Building relationships
Spiritual direction
Spiritual friendship
Stewardship
Spiritual service through spiritual gifts

Earlier in his book, Rumford suggests that the shaping of the soul is coordinate with alignment with God's purposes. He says,

---

12. Rumford, *Soul Shaping*, 430–31.

"As we align ourselves with God's purposes—what he designed us to do and to be from the beginning of creation—our lives will take on the beautiful shape of Christ-like people, who show the world what God is like."[13]

Most writers on the subject of personal evangelism assume that the same Spirit who produces life-changing fruit (Gal 5:22–23) also empowers one to witness (Acts 1:8). Jim Petersen sees the need for a witness to have what he calls congruence between God's ways and his ways. He says:

> A congruent life is the secret of naturalness in communication. And naturalness is the secret of attracting rather than repelling with our witness. On the other hand, when there are incongruities in our lives we usually have to resort to devices or gimmicks to get our message across.[14]

Factor Four—Formal Training in Evangelism

The existence of numerous formal evangelism training programs suggests that the presence and success of such programs influence the practice of OPE. D. James Kennedy, the founder of Evangelism Explosion, argues that the key ingredient for involving lay people in evangelism is "on-the-job training."[15] A survey of 250 congregations of the Christian church summarizes eight points for growing churches. Two of those points relate to formal training in evangelism: "7. There is a need for providing help in setting goals and implementing them. 8. There is a need for leadership training in the area of renewal/evangelism."[16] Whether or not such programs encourage the practice of OPE is yet to be determined. My own experience in training others is that formal training encourages evangelism while the training is in process, but that the factors that drive OPE are deeper.

13. Rumford, *Soul Shaping*, 101.
14. Petersen, *Evangelism as a Lifestyle*, 79.
15. Kennedy, *Evangelism Explosion*, 6.
16. Miller, *Evangelism's Open Secrets*, 61.

On the other hand, contrary to the suggestion of most literature that formal training has positive effects, is the conclusion of Juan M. Isais suggesting that the decline in personal evangelism is in proportion to the amount of formal training. He asserts:

> The believers lose their natural ability to evangelize in direct proportion to their involvement in the technology of the church regarding personal evangelism. In other words, the more we train them in evangelism, they less they do it.[17]

Isais's remarks are based upon his experience as founder and director of the Latin American Mission of Mexico and as an instructor and participant in the Lausanne Congress on World Evangelism since its inception. He argues for an intensely personal evangelistic approach driven by what he calls "first love" instead of formal methodologies. He states:

> In others words, the number of methods of communicating the gospel of salvation are multiplied as many times as people are willing to share and have opportunity to do so.[18]

Formal training is a relative factor but not an absolute one in OPE.

Factor Five—Theological Commitments

One's theological commitments may influence one's practice of OPE. For instance, Millard Erickson asserts that in the past, evangelism was motivated by the strength of one's theology about the eternal suffering of the lost:

> Traditionally, evangelism was motivated at least in part by the conviction that all must be reached with the good news of the gospel, because all are lost and are under God's condemnation for their sins. Now, however, some

---

17. Isais, *Other Evangelism*, 16.
18. Isais, *Other Evangelism*, 36.

view the status of the unevangelized differently. Perhaps those who have not heard the gospel are not lost, it is argued. They may be savingly related to God on the basis of the knowledge all humans can obtain from the study of nature and of themselves.

Perhaps those who have not heard the gospel in this life will have opportunity to hear it after they die, and such a presentation might well be more convincing than that of an ordinary human evangelist. Thus, if not already "saved," they may well be in the future, even without human instrumentality. Rather than bringing about their salvation, efforts at evangelism and missions may serve only to bring about their condemnation.[19]

Another writer, William Crocker, has documented the evangelical divergence on this subject.[20] If one admits that the description of hell, even if accepting it as imagery and a condescension to human limitations with the terminology employed, depicts an awful reality that supersedes one's finite imagination, then one will be careful to never speak of hell without gravity and compassion for those who are lost. It seems likely that one would be gripped and grieved by the fact that millions are perishing without Christ and that something dreadful awaits them.

J. I. Packer expresses another example of how one's theological commitments may affect one's evangelism practice. He asserts that one's understanding of effectual calling should lead to boldness, patience, and prayerfulness in evangelism.[21] He concludes with regard to divine sovereignty that it does "undergird evangelism, and uphold the evangelist, by creating a hope of success that could not otherwise be entertained."[22]

Other examples of theological commitments that encourage evangelism are the understanding of an intertrinitarian covenant that guarantees a bride for the Son, the privilege and reward of working with the Father in a harvest that is guaranteed to be

19. Erickson, "Fate of Those," 14.
20. Crockett, *Four Views on Hell*.
21. Packer, *Evangelism and Sovereignty*, 118–24.
22. Packer, *Evangelism and Sovereignty*, 125.

successful, the knowledge that God is glorified in evangelism, and the belief of the uniqueness of the atonement provided by Jesus Christ. Sinclair Ferguson suggests that Paul's endurance in his gospel ministry gained impetus because of his doctrine:

> What sustained Paul under these pressures? There is only one answer. He had a vital knowledge of the character of God, the nature of God's ways, and the indwelling power of the Holy Spirit. His life was characterized by the power which the truth released in his experience.[23]

Factor Six—Evangelism as a Gift

Another factor that surfaced in the literature search was the effect that one's understanding of evangelism either as a gift or a responsibility has on the practice of OPE. While the New Testament speaks of a specialized gift of evangelists (Eph 4:11), it also speaks of the common responsibility of evangelism (Acts 1:8). Does the concept of special giftedness for evangelism detract from a churchwide sense of responsibility for OPE? Is the understanding of evangelism as a spiritual gift important to those who practice OPE?

Larry Thiel, when challenging students to be involved in evangelism, asks four questions that represent this idea of a specialization in evangelism:

> Are you someone who has to be around not-yet-believing seekers or else you would go into withdrawal? Are you somewhat spontaneous and often late for meetings because you just can't help but get into evangelistic conversations? Do you ever get a weird urge in the middle of a large group meeting to rebuke everyone who hasn't led another person to Christ in the last twenty-four hours? Do you hate going to evangelistic events because you think you could do a better job preaching the gospel than the celebrity evangelist who has been invited?[24]

---

23. Ferguson, *Christian Life*, 5.
24. Thiel, "Are You a Gifted Evangelist," 1.

After asking these questions, Thiel then makes a statement that could easily lead some to conclude that they do not have a gift of evangelism. Thiel asks: "If you can answer yes to any of the above questions then you may be an evangelist at heart—and you may even have the spiritual gift of evangelism."[25] Teaching such as this may give impetus to the idea that some Christians practice evangelism, and others do not.

In this regard, many spiritual gift questionnaires identify evangelism as one of the possible gifts. This understanding of evangelism as a spiritual gift leads those who score low in the evangelism category to conclude that they do not have the gift of evangelism and therefore have no personal responsibility for evangelism.

Factor Seven—Adaptability to Culture

Mission literature has for a long time recognized the need for sensitivity to culture in evangelism. However, until recently the evangelism literature assumed a somewhat monocultural society here in the United States. James Engel, in his seminal writing on reaching a harvest and on communication theory, set the stage for evangelism's call to understand culture.[26]

The possibility exists today that one's ability to understand and adjust to changing cultures may be a factor in the practice of OPE. For instance, Christians may become uncomfortable living in a postmodern world and may feel incapable of communicating to a changing culture. Rick Richardson confesses the crisis he faced as he began to talk to postmoderns:

> It was a crisis of inadequacy, of fear of rejection, and feeling powerless to influence them toward Christ. They were asking questions I wasn't prepared to answer; they no longer seemed interested in the questions I was prepared to answer.[27]

25. Thiel, "Are You a Gifted Evangelist," 1.
26. Engel, *Contemporary Christian Communication*.
27. Richardson, *Evangelism Outside the Box*, 41.

However, because of his commitment to OPE, he pursued a way to communicate the gospel.

Because the new world in which we live is suspicious about claims to certainty and objective truth, a greater degree of humility is needed in communicating the gospel of Jesus Christ. Is it necessary that those who practice OPE adjust to this changing climate? Brian McLaren insightfully describes the disposition needed at such a time as this:

> As we move to the other side, our greatest enemy will not be our ignorance; it will be our unteachability. It won't be what we don't know that threatens us; it will be what we do know. We know too much—so much that we can't learn how much we need to learn.[28]

Ministry in a postmodern world requires more humility about our theological certainties. Humility does not entail the diminishing of theological affirmation, but removes the arrogance and unteachability that often is associated with Christians.

Along with humility will come the practice of fairness where, as McLaren suggests, "we need to be more careful about applying a degree of scrutiny to others . . . that we cannot ourselves withstand."[29] It is important that those who continue in OPE understand and adjust to the culture in which they share the gospel. Perhaps the inability or the unwillingness to adapt to changing cultures inhibits the practice of OPE.

Factor Eight—Community/Accountability

Finally, it appears that there is some relationship between accountability and one's involvement in OPE. By accountability, I mean being in community with others who are involved in evangelism. Michael Wilkins notes the importance of accountability in following Jesus Christ:

---

28. McLaren, *Church on the Other Side*, 38–39.
29. McLaren, *Church on the Other Side*, 176.

> Notice how often we find the disciples in a group, whether it is the Twelve, or the group of women, or the Seventy being sent out two by two. Very seldom do we find them alone. We need other disciples. Growth in our developing walk with Jesus will be, in part, proportional to our accountability to others.[30]

Rick Richardson also testifies to the powerful influence of working with others in evangelism:

> I was shocked at the impact of that team in my life. I turned from evangelistic mouse to powerhouse in a week, just because of the encouragement and spiritual nurture of that group of people.[31]

Summary

I conclude on the basis of observations and research that each of the preceding factors are of some importance in the lives of those who practice OPE. The factors that appear to be most essential are 1) definition of evangelism, 2) spiritual authenticity, and 3) theological commitment.

---

30. Wilkins, *Following the Master*, 143.
31. Richardson, *Evangelism Outside the Box*, 63.

3

Research Undergirding the Eight Factors

My Doctor of Ministry project was to discover common factors in the lives of Christians who practice OPE. I asked evangelical pastor friends to identify those in their congregations who practiced OPE. The respondents filled out a survey which indicated their priority of the eight factors (Appendix A).

Of the eight factors that surfaced from my biblical-theological study and my survey of previous literature, five factors proved to be a contributing influence by a majority when tallying the "strongly agree" responses (Table 5.1). Two of the factors appeared to be negligible when respondents were asked about their having a strong agreement. Only 12 percent strongly agreed that one's personality was an influence, and a mere 7 percent said the same about having a gift of evangelism. One of the factors, cultural sensitivity, had the support of 27 percent strongly agreeing, making it more difficult to evaluate this factor at this point.

Ongoing Personal Evangelism

	Number	Percentage
Definition	64	88%
Authenticity	58	78%
Theological Commitments	46	64%
Formal Training	40	54%
Community/ Accountability	36	49%
Cultural Sensitivity	20	27%
Personality	9	12%
Gift of Evangelism	5	7%

Table 5.1 Strongly Agreeing

However, when combining all the agreeing responses, though having a gift of evangelism still remained negligible at 16 percent, the influence of one's personality rose to 47 percent, and cultural sensitivity rose to 66 percent (Table 5.1).

Research Undergirding the Eight Factors

	Number	Percentage
Definition	72	98%
Authenticity	70	94%
Theological Commitments	65	88%
Community/ Accountability	57	77%
Formal Training	51	70%
Cultural Sensitivity	49	66%
Personality	34	46%
Gift of Evangelism	12	16%

Table 5.2 Combined Agreeing

Nevertheless, this still means that less than half of all respondents saw personality as an influential factor in their practice of OPE. The data also signifies that 74 percent of all respondents disagreed in some measure with the idea that the gift of evangelism influences their practice of OPE (Table 5.3).

Ongoing Personal Evangelism

	Strongly Agree	Combined Agree
Definition	86%	98%
Authenticity	78%	94%
Theological Commitments	62%	88%
Community/ Accountability	49%	77%
Formal Training	54%	70%
Cultural Sensitivity	27%	66%
Personality	12%	47%
Gift of Evangelism	7%	16%

Table 5.3 Agreement and Strong Disagreement

Consequently, over two-thirds of the respondents support six factors as having varying degrees of influence on their practice of OPE. Three of these six factors stand unequivocally as a powerful triad that influences OPE (Table 5.4). They are:

1. defining evangelism as a verbal sharing of the gospel
2. commitment to authentic Christian living
3. theological commitments

Research Undergirding the Eight Factors

	Number	Percentage
Definition	72	98%
Authenticity	70	94%
Theological Commitments	65	88%

Table 5.4 The Powerful Triad

This data supports the literature and biblical-theological study on the prominence of these three factors. The combination of these three factors appears to be a predominant influence in the lives of those who practice OPE.

To a lesser degree, yet notable enough, was the strength of approval for the other three factors (Table 5.5):

1. formal training at 54 percent (70 percent combined)
2. accountability/community at 49 percent (77 percent combined)
3. adaptability to culture at 27 percent (66 percent combined)

	Number	Percentage
Community/Accountability	57	77%
Formal Training	51	70%
Cultural Sensitivity	49	66%

Table 5.5 Contributing Factors

Though the biblical-theological study did not directly show the importance of formal training, the data shows that over two-thirds of the respondents agree that it was important. This conclusion does not necessarily refute Isais's claim that formal training diminishes evangelism.[1] However, it does reveal that those who were formally trained and who continued in personal evangelism considered their formal training as important. What Isais may have observed is that formal training, when not accompanied by the powerful triad, does not produce OPE.

The priority ordering of the factors yields similar conclusions. The powerful triad mentioned above again stands as a clear priority in the pursuit of OPE (Table 5.6). The pursuit of authentic Christianity receives the most first-place choices (40) and combined first-, second-, and third-place choices (61). Theological commitment was second for first-place choices (13), but was third for combined choices (47). The definition of evangelism was third for first-place choices (7), but was second for combined choices (52).

	First Choice		Combined First, Second, and Third Choices	
	Number	Percentage	Number	Percentage
Authenticity	40	54%	61	82%
Theological Commitments	13	18%	47	64%
Definition	7	9%	52	70%

Table 5.6 Three Highest Priorities

The pursuit of authentic Christianity stands clearly as the first-place choice, with the definition of evangelism and theological

---

1. Isais, *Other Evangelism*, 16.

Research Undergirding the Eight Factors

commitments following closely. The primary influence of all three of these factors again surfaces in both the first and the second section.

The combined choices for the gift of evangelism as first, second, or third priority (6) again indicates its relative insignificance.

In summary, considering the results of the survey, the importance of the eight factors could be stated as follows:

1. Understanding evangelism in its original sense as an intentional process that includes a verbal sharing of the gospel of Christ is important in the practice of OPE.
2. Personality is neither a limiting or determinative factor in the practice of OPE.
3. Pursuit of authentic discipleship and Christian living is essential in the lives of those who practice OPE.
4. Formal training is a powerful factor in the practice of OPE, when coupled with the powerful triad.
5. Various theological commitments strongly influence one's practice of OPE.
6. It is one's belief regarding evangelism as a responsibility, rather than as a gift, that affects one's OPE.
7. For most of those involved in OPE, the ability to discern and adapt to changing culture is an important factor.
8. Though some may be quite capable of doing evangelism as lone rangers, the overwhelming majority sees accountability as an important factor in the practice of OPE.

4

Implications of the Eight Factors

As a result of the research into OPE, some of the implications are as follows:

1. More teaching and writing needs to be done to clarify the definition of evangelism.
2. More emphasis needs to be made on the role of the Spirit in utilizing diverse personalities.
3. A greater focus on authentic Christian living and the call to discipleship needs to take place.
4. Greater commitment to developing culturally relevant evangelistic training should be in place.
5. Greater attention needs to be given to teaching theological commitments that have implications for evangelism.
6. There needs to be more clarity on evangelism as Christian responsibility, as opposed to evangelism as a spiritual gift.
7. More attention should be given to understanding changing cultures, especially postmodernism.
8. More attention should be given to developing accountability in relationships and structures that promote OPE.

Implications of the Eight Factors

Each of the above implications is supported in varying degrees by the research. Several more implications also arise. The following discussion relates future implications to the eight conclusions from the survey results.

Understanding evangelism in its original sense as an intentional process that includes a verbal sharing of the gospel of Christ is important in the practice of OPE.

It is clear that a precise definition of evangelism is an integral factor for those who practice OPE. At the outset I offered the following definition of OPE: the regular, personal, and intentional practice of building relationships with non-believers, and verbally sharing the gospel of Jesus Christ with the intent to call for a commitment. Though there are many things that precede, accompany, and assist the building of relationships with non-believers, evangelism should include in its definition a verbal sharing of the gospel of Jesus Christ with the intent to call for a commitment.

As I read literature on evangelism, it becomes apparent how easily the definition of evangelism becomes confused. In Jim Petersen's very fine book *Evangelism as a Lifestyle*, Petersen unfortunately confuses the definition. Listen to his explanation:

> We will be developing two primary modes of evangelism in the Scriptures. They are:
>
> 1. The *proclamation* of the gospel: an *action* through which the non-Christian receives a clear statement of the essential message.
>
> 2. The *affirmation* of the gospel: a *process* of modeling and explaining the Christian message.[1]

What Petersen defines as the proclamation of the gospel approaches a basic definition of evangelism. However, in his second point on affirmation, he confuses authentic Christian living and

---

1. Petersen, *Evangelism as a Lifestyle*, 22; italics in original.

verbal proclamation. It appears that for him, evangelism is both the modeling and the proclamation of the message. Though both are necessary as biblical responsibilities, they do not together constitute a definition of evangelism. This critique does not seek to diminish the vital role of authentic Christianity, but only to distinguish the modeling of Christianity from the definition of evangelism.

Not only is the definition of evangelism amalgamated with other things, but also sometimes an author assumes that readers have a clear definition. A fine book on relating to people in a postmodern culture is *Reinventing Evangelism* by Donald C. Posterski. However, the book unfortunately offers no stated definition of evangelism. The closest statement to a definition is when Poterski describes what he calls meaning-makers:

> Meaning-makers are people who make sense of life, people who make sense of God, people whose lives ring with clarity in the midst of contemporary ambiguity, people who have integrity, people who reside in today's world revealing with their living and their lips that Jesus' death is the source of vital life.[2]

It is not clear that Posterski intends this to be his definition of evangelism. However, if it is his definition, then again the definition of evangelism is commingled with another factor of evangelism, i.e., authentic Christian living. It appears that a similar confusion exists in much of the lifestyle evangelism corpus of literature.

A danger of not having a clear definition is that those who read much of the popular evangelistic literature may practice many of the good things that have been confused with evangelism without ever arriving at the point of verbal proclamation. Yet, they may believe they are involved in evangelism. Hospitality, social work, serving others, etc. are good accompaniments to evangelism, but there is no evangelism without a verbal proclamation of the gospel.

Another danger, on the other hand, is that one may hold a correct definition of evangelism and be involved in verbally

---

2. Posterski, *Reinventing Evangelism*, 15.

proclaiming the gospel, yet may be woefully ineffective, because the other factors are not evident.

Literature for evangelism and training in evangelistic method needs to start with a clear definition and then needs to reiterate that definition vociferously. Richard Mouw emphasizes the importance of cognitive content in the evangelistic task:

> Evangelism is the announcement of the "good news" of God's gracious offer of salvation in Jesus Christ. If there is no articulation of the "news," then the evangelistic task has not been properly pursued.[3]

Personality is neither a limiting or determinative factor in the practice of OPE.

Since there are diverse personalities involved in evangelism, we must ask, how can we diminish the focus on training processes that favor a particular personality type, and how can we show people that they can work within their God-given personality makeup?

One of the most popular evangelism training programs is *Evangelism Explosion*. One of its weaknesses is that its style of learning and on-the-job training is geared more for a confrontational personality type. Having been certified in *Evangelism Explosion* and having trained others for years, this researcher concluded that specific material was geared toward a personality type that represented a small percentage of a congregation. Therefore, its success as a churchwide training program had inherent limitations. The recent revision of that program has worked hard to incorporate more of a relational, lifestyle focus in evangelism, expanding its appeal to a greater number within a congregation.

Contrariwise, one of the strong points of the *Becoming a Contagious Christian* approach to evangelism is its recognition that evangelism is everyone's responsibility and that evangelism can be effectively practiced regardless of personality type. This training program talks about personality types using the terminology of

---

3. Mouw, "Evangelism," 176.

style or approach. Six styles are set forth: the confrontational, the intellectual, the testimonial, the interpersonal, the invitational, and the serving.[4] Though there is something self-limiting about suggesting only six styles, the training program at least recognizes the diversity of human personality makeup. The section on styles concludes with these words: "The important thing to know is that most contagious Christians are those who've learned to work within the design God has given them."[5]

In the future development of evangelism training, more consideration should be given to work of the Spirit in empowering every Christian for witnessing, regardless of personality type. Perhaps a biblical study of how the Spirit used different personalities such as Paul, Apollos, Peter, John, and others to accomplish his work would encourage more dependence on the Holy Spirit.

Pursuit of authentic discipleship and Christian living is essential in the lives of those who practice OPE.

There is a strong correlation between the practice of OPE and a commitment to spiritual growth and authenticity in Christian living. Those involved in OPE testify to their desire to nurture a growing relationship with Jesus Christ through maintaining a vital devotional life.

Since those involved in OPE see their involvement in OPE as a matter of obedience, it is fair to conclude that these respondents saw their involvement in evangelism in a similar way to which they viewed their involvement in reading the Bible and prayer. They understood that both maintaining a devotional life and involvement in OPE are important in the pursuit of authentic Christian living.

The New Testament supports the conclusion that faithful witness is a matter of spirituality. It is a natural by-product of the

---

4. Hybels and Mittleberg, *Becoming a Contagious Christian*, 122–32.
5. Hybels and Mittleberg, *Becoming a Contagious Christian*, 132.

Implications of the Eight Factors

Spirit's work (Acts 1:8), in a similar way that ethical behavior is the fruit of the Spirit's work (Gal 5:22).

It would be fair to infer the need to focus on spiritual development in the pursuit of multiplying those involved in OPE. Vitality in one's walk with the Lord is logically a factor in one's practice of OPE. The evangelist is essentially a witness—one who testifies to what he knows and has experienced.

This reminds us that OPE is not simply the Christian practice of speaking the gospel, but it is something that reflects their understanding and experience of the gospel. The message of the cross is not only the message to save sinners (Rom 1:16) but also the message at the heart of spiritual growth (Rom 6). To those who are saved, the message of the cross is the power of God (1 Cor 1:18). From a biblical perspective, deep appreciation for the death of Christ is at the core of motivating those who are involved in OPE.

> For Christ's love compels us, because we are convinced that one died for all, and therefore all died. And he died for all, that those who live should no longer live for themselves but for him who died for them and was raised again. (2 Cor 5:14–15)

A question we need to ask and answer is "How do we teach and train spiritual disciplines that are rooted in the gospel and that nurture one's involvement in OPE?" What is needed is more than the development of spiritual disciplines. The need is for spiritual disciplines and evangelism to be spoken in the same breath. The need is for one's experience of the gospel to move beyond any type of deeper life experience that does not produce OPE.

Since there are a host of believers who practice spiritual disciplines yet do not get involved in OPE, it appears that this factor needs the mixture of the other factors to catalyze it for evangelism.

Formal training is a powerful factor in the practice of OPE, when coupled with the powerful triad.

Admittedly, I look at this factor with a bit of personal ambivalence. Having been involved in training others for twenty-five years, I had become somewhat disillusioned with the effectiveness of formal training in producing OPE. I had concluded that it was not vital and necessary. However, research shows that those involved in OPE see formal training as having a vital influence. My perspective is that the influence is effective when coupled with a clear definition of evangelism, spiritual authenticity, and theological commitment.

The implication is that formal training must be coupled with the other factors to be effective in nurturing OPE. I now understand that there may be deficiencies in the training by not focusing on all the factors, or there may be deficiencies in the trainee, but formal training is an important factor in evangelism. A suggested format for training is in Appendix B.

Various theological commitments strongly influence one's practice of OPE.

Since those involved in OPE hold theological commitments related to the gospel, it stands to reason that understanding the terms of the gospel, including the plight of sinners without Christ, the exclusivity of the work of Christ, and obedience to the command to evangelize, is of great importance.

Those involved in OPE have a degree of clarity about the gospel message and the mandate to share it with the world. Again, Matt 28:18–20 was the text most often cited (33x) as expressing one's theological commitment. Perhaps this text needs more attention, exposition, repetition, and memorization. The data suggests the need for evangelism training to include a biblical-theological survey of personal evangelism and a clear understanding of the gospel.

John K. Barrett offers a perceptive analysis of the negative impact that bad theology, such as inclusivist theology (which intends to open the door of heaven to those who have not heard the gospel) has on evangelism. After discussing certain strengths of inclusivist theology, such as an emphasis on the love of God, he then exposes its inherent weaknesses in "divorcing the ontological from the epistemological necessity of Christ." He states:

> These weaknesses, individually and together, suggest that it is simply "wishful thinking" on behalf of hard inclusivists to assert that an unqualified inclusivist theology can maintain the traditional call to evangelism."[6]

A clear theology on the exclusive nature of the gospel and the mandate for evangelism necessarily undergird OPE.

It is one's belief regarding evangelism as a responsibility, rather than as a gift, that affects one's OPE.

Since research shows that the gift of evangelism has little bearing on those involved in OPE, a few steps should be taken. First, spiritual gift questionnaires should delete the category of gift of evangelism. It clearly is not a factor in the practice of OPE and may be misleading. Those who take a spiritual gift test that concludes they do not have a gift of evangelism may be dissuaded from evangelism.

Secondly, clearer exposition refuting an alleged gift of evangelism and distinguishing the office of evangelist (Eph 4:11) is needed. What is needed is to recognize that all believers are commanded to evangelize as a matter of obedient Christian living, while some believers are additionally called to an office of evangelism as a matter of vocation.

---

6. J. Barrett, "Does Inclusivist Theology," 244.

For most of those involved in OPE, the ability to discern and adapt to changing culture is an important factor.

There is always a need to develop evangelistic training that is culturally relevant and a need to understand the current movement in our culture toward postmodernism. An evangelistic approach needed to communicate the gospel to a postmodern culture is one that listens to the culture, presents a storyline theology, maintains ongoing conversation, gently seeks commitment, and stays connected with community.

Kevin Graham Ford suggests that listening to culture enables us to see where the Christian worldview intersects at a few places. He points out four junctures where biblical Christianity can intersect with postmodernism:

1. Postmoderns accept the existence of the supernatural;
2. Postmoderns reject the idea of an autonomous self and see themselves as parts of a larger whole;
3. Postmoderns seek a communal reality;
4. Postmoderns pursue a responsible stewardship of the environment.[7]

These junctures offer starting points for conversation about Jesus.

The presentation of the gospel should be an incremental, ongoing conversation that moves people through the storyline of the Bible. An example of an evangelistic message that uses a storyline approach is the following modification of the *Two Ways to Live* presentation.[8]

1. God is the loving creator of the world.
   He created the world.
   He created us to be rulers of the world under him.
   (Gen 1:1; John 1:1–3; Col 1:16–18)

---

7. Ford, *Jesus for a New Generation*, 124–25.
8. Payne and Jensen, *Two Ways to Live*.

Implications of the Eight Factors

2. But, we all have become corrupted, having rebelled in seeking to live life our own way.
   (Gen 3; Rom 3:10–12, Isa 53:6)

3. God continually seeks out rebels through his Word (covenant) and calls them to a relationship with himself.
   This relationship requires a response to his Word.
   Faith in God's Word is the single requirement. Faith implies obedience.
   (Gen 3:9; Gen 12:1; 15:6; Eph 2:8–9)
   Transition: The ultimate call is through the cross of Jesus Christ.

4. God, through the cross of Christ, redeems those who have violated his Word (covenant breakers).
   (1 Pet 3:18; Gal 3:13)

5. God gathers those who believe his Word (covenant-keepers) into his community.
   (Acts 2:41–42)

6. God rewards the faithful (covenant keepers) and judges the unbelieving (covenant breakers) in the end.
   (Matt 25:46; Rom 14:12; 2 Cor 10:5; Rev 20)
   Do you sense that God has been seeking you? Are you willing to believe that God has solved your sin problem through the death and resurrection of Jesus Christ? Today, will you obey his Word by putting your faith in Jesus Christ and choosing to submit to him?

The intent of presenting the gospel in a biblical-theological way is as follows:

1. To make clear the complicated scope of biblical revelation, which we often assume

2. To present a biblical message that is both content-full and all-embracing

3. To be able to converse with biblical illiterates by setting forth a biblical worldview

Another helpful outline of the gospel is the credo for the New Life for All movement in Africa and Latin America.

Ongoing Personal Evangelism

1. God created all people for life.
2. People, in their sin, have forfeited life.
3. God came in Christ to offer people new life.
4. People can receive this new life by turning
   - from their sins
   - to Christ in trust and obedience
   - to the community of new life
5. People knowing new life are called to be faithful in all relationships.[9]

Bringing a postmodern to commitment is a work of the Holy Spirit utilizing the means of both the Word of God and Christian community. Again, Kevin Graham Ford offers helpful guidelines in bringing a postmodern to commitment. Some of his suggestions are summarized as follows:

1. Focus on Christianity as a relationship, not a religion.
2. Emphasize freedom in Christ, not rules and structures.
3. Emphasize Christian community, not institutions.
4. Emphasize how meaning and purpose for existing in human society are found in Christ.
5. Build trust through authentic Christian living.
6. Build trust through unconditional acceptance.
7. Build genuine friendship that is not only evangelistically oriented.
8. Be sensitive to cultural issues that are important to postmoderns.[10]

As we continue to engage in conversation with our culture, we should analyze and dissect our culture and then revise our theological expressions and evangelistic training so that they speak the language of our culture. We will then continue in conversation

---

9. Hunter, *How to Reach*, 87.
10. Ford, *Jesus for a New Generation*, 148–49.

Implications of the Eight Factors

with pre-Christians with humility and sensitivity toward the goal of sharing with them the gospel of Jesus Christ.

> **Though some may be quite capable of doing evangelism as lone rangers, the overwhelming majority sees accountability as an important factor in the practice of OPE.**

In an ideal world, every believer would be self-motivated to practice OPE on his own. However, the reality is that the presence of sin necessitates the need for accountability and encouragement. The Bible's primary method of accountability is within the body-life of a church where the "one another" commands are taken seriously. Ronald Johnson suggests that one of the problems with OPE is that many churches train witnesses but do not provide ongoing support. He says:

> People who try to share their faith on a regular basis need the support that a group can offer. They need opportunities to debrief. They need to be able to talk with others about roadblocks they encounter in the witnessing process.[11]

Encouraging accountability and providing creative mechanisms of accountability are challenges that need to be taken seriously. The *Evangelism Explosion* training program of meeting over a course of thirteen weeks and establishing teams of three is a good example of a system that works, at least for the thirteen-week period. Whether through evangelism teams or evangelism partners or triads, most people function more consistently with accountability. The current popularity of cell groups provides an ideal mechanism for accountability, if the group members will take OPE seriously. Jim Petersen notes this important opportunity for cell groups. In regard to cell groups, he says the following:

> They also proved to be an ideal environment for ongoing witness among peers. We learned that a small group will

---

11. Johnson, *How Will They Hear*, 43.

soon become unhealthily introspective if it neglects this dimension of corporate and individual witness.[12]

Our ongoing conversation with pre-Christians will be most effective when the community of faith undergirds it, so that the evangelistic conversation is not an individual effort. Perhaps the ancient Celtic Christians best exemplified the value of evangelizing as a community. They did this by "relating to the people of a settlement; identifying with the people; engaging in friendship, conversation, ministry, and witness."[13] George Hunter proceeds to note John Finney's observations that "the Celts believed in 'the importance of the team. A group can pray and think together. They inspire and encourage each other. The single entrepreneur is too easily prey to self-doubt and loss of vision.'"[14]

Doing evangelism in the context of community properly reflects our commitment to community as based on Trinitarian theology, and it addresses the present cultural desire to belong to a group before believing.

Summary

The conclusion is that there are common factors that influence one's practice of OPE and that those factors can be taught and nurtured. Those factors are not unique to an elite group within the body of Christ, but are possible in the lives of all believers.

The three primary factors are a clear definition of evangelism, pursuing spiritual authenticity, and having strong theological commitment. To a lesser degree, yet still important, are formal training, cultural adaptability, and community/accountability.

The hope and prayer of this author is that every believer will accept the privilege and responsibility of personal evangelism and that this book may encourage an understanding and a pursuit of these contributing factors in their lives.

---

12. Petersen, *Church Without Walls*, 201.
13. Ford, *Jesus for a New Generation*, 47.
14. Ford, *Jesus for a New Generation*, 47.

Appendix A

Evangelism Questionnaire

YOU HAVE BEEN IDENTIFIED as someone who regularly seeks to share the gospel of Jesus Christ with others. If you feel that this assessment is true of you, then please proceed.

Research has identified certain possible factors as existing in part or in whole in the lives of people who practice OPE. By OPE, I mean the regular, personal, and intentional practice of building relationships with non-believers with the goal of sharing the gospel of Jesus Christ. Would you please indicate the strength of your agreement or disagreement with the following statements, using this scale?

5—Strongly Agree 4—Somewhat Agree
3—Undecided
2—Somewhat Disagree 1—Strongly Disagree

1. I understand that evangelism necessitates verbally sharing the gospel of Christ with someone who is lost.

    1   2   3   4   5

2. My personality and psychological makeup are a determining factor in my practice of OPE.

    1   2   3   4   5

Appendix A

3. There is a direct correlation between my commitment to share the gospel and my commitment to personal spiritual growth in authentic Christian living.

    1   2   3   4   5

4. Formal evangelism training (such as EE, lifestyle evangelism, etc.) has been a determinative factor in my practice of OPE.

    1   2   3   4   5

5. I am conscious of specific theological commitments that directly influence my practice of OPE.

    1   2   3   4   5

6. Understanding that I may have a gift of evangelism is a determinative motivation in my practice of OPE. (If you are more inclined to believe in evangelism as a responsibility rather than as a gift, your answer would be 1.)

    1   2   3   4   5

7. My willingness and ability to understand and adapt to changing cultures impacts my practice of OPE.

    1   2   3   4   5

8. Being in community with others who are involved in OPE influences my practice of OPE.

    1   2   3   4   5

Section Two

Assuming that these eight factors are somewhat related to the practice of OPE, would you number them from 1 to 8 in the order of their priority of influence in your life. 1 is the highest priority and 8 is the lowest.

_____ My formal training

_____ My pursuit of authentic Christianity

Evangelism Questionnaire

____ My personality and psychological makeup

____ My understanding that evangelism is a gift

____ My theological commitments

____ My understanding that evangelism involves a verbal sharing of the gospel

____ My willingness and ability to understand and to adapt to changing culture

____ My accountability to others involved in evangelism

Section Three

Please answer the following questions briefly.

1. What formal evangelistic training have you had?

2. What three words would you use to describe your personality?

3. What are the two main practices in your life that promote spiritual growth?

4. What specific theological commitments influence your practice of evangelism?

Appendix B

Ongoing Personal Evangelism
Training Outline

Training Session One	*The Definition of Personal Evangelism*
	This session will show the confusion that surrounds the definition of evangelism and will argue for a definition of evangelism that necessitates a verbal proclamation.
Training Session Two	*The Theology of Personal Evangelism*
	This session will give a biblical-theological background for evangelism and will define the content of the gospel.
Training Session Three	*The Responsibility for Personal Evangelism*
	This session will establish evangelism as every Christian's call. Also, it will discuss the role of human personality and the Holy Spirit in evangelism.

Ongoing Personal Evangelism

Training Session Four	*The Need for Spiritual Authenticity in Personal Evangelism*
	This session will develop the need for spiritual authenticity and recommend processes for achieving it.
Training Session Five	*The Changing Climate for Personal Evangelism*
	This session will focus on how we relate an unchanging message to a changing culture. Special attention will be given to evangelism in a postmodern culture.
Training Session Six	*The Practice of Personal Evangelism (1)*
	This session will focus on several methods of entering into conversations that lead to the gospel.
Training Session Seven	*The Practice of Personal Evangelism (2)*
	This session will focus on methods of communicating the content of the gospel.
Training Session Eight	*The Need for Accountability in Personal Evangelism*
	This session will show the need of accountability in the lives of those who practice OPE. It will suggest ways in which accountability may take place.

Bibliography

Arndt, W. F. and Gingrich, F. W. *A Greek-English Lexicon of the New Testament and Other Early Christian Literature*. Chicago: University of Chicago Press, 1957.
Barrett, David B. *Evangelize: A Historical Survey of the Concept*. Birmingham: New Hope, 1987.
Barrett, John K. "Does Inclusivist Theology Undermine Evangelism?" *Evangelical Quarterly* (July 1988) 219-45.
Best, Ernest. *Disciples and Discipleship: Studies in the Gospel According to Mark*. Edinburgh: T. & T. Clark, 1986.
Bowers, W. P. "Mission." In *Dictionary of Paul and His Letters*, edited by Gerald F. Hawthorne et al., 935-49. Downers Grove, IL: Intervarsity, 1993.
Bruce, A. B. *The Training of the Twelve*. Grand Rapids: Kregel, 1988.
Creswell, John W. *Research and Design: Qualitative and Quantitative Approaches*. Thousand Oaks, CA: Sage, 1994.
Crockett, William, ed. *Four Views on Hell*. Grand Rapids: Zondervan, 1996.
Converse, Jean M. and Presser, Stanley. *Survey Questions: Handcrafting the Standardized Questionnaire*. Newbury Park, CA: Sage, 1986.
Conybeare, W. J. and J. S. Howson. *The Life and Epistles of St. Paul*. 2 vols. New York: Charles Scribner, 1864.
Engel, James F. *Contemporary Christian Communication*. Nashville: Thomas Nelson, 1979.
———. *What's Gone Wrong with the Harvest?* Grand Rapids: Zondervan, 1975.
Erickson, Millard J. "The Fate of Those Who Never Hear." *Bibliotheca Sacra* 152 (Jan.-Mar. 1995) 3-15.
Ferguson, Sinclair B. *The Christian Life: A Doctrinal Introduction*. Carlisle, PA: Banner of Truth, 1981.
Ford, Kevin Graham. *Jesus for a New Generation*. Downers Grove, IL: Intervarsity, 1995.
Freeman, Hal. "The Great Commission and the New Testament: An Exegesis of Matthew 28:19-20." *Southern Baptist Journal of Theology* 4 (Winter 1997) 14-23.

Bibliography

Harding, Susan F. "Convicted by the Holy Spirit: The Rhetoric of Fundamental Baptist Conversion." *American Ethnologist* 14 (Feb. 1987) 167-81.

Harrison, R. K. "The Pastor's Use of the Old Testament, Part Two: Credibility and Enthusiasm in Preaching the Old Testament." *Bibliotheca Sacra* 146 (Apr.-June 1988) 123-31.

Hull, Bill. *Jesus Christ, Disciplemaker*. Minneapolis: Evangelical Free Church of America, 1984.

Hunsberger, George R. "Is there Biblical Warrant for Evangelism?" *Interpretation* 48, no. 2 (Apr. 1995) 131-44.

Hunter, George G., III. *The Celtic Way of Evangelism*. Nashville: Abingdon, 2000.

———. *How to Reach Secular People*. Nashville: Abingdon, 1992.

Hybels, Bill and Mark Mittleberg. *Becoming a Contagious Christian*. Grand Rapids: Zondervan, 1992.

Isais, M. Juan. *The Other Evangelism*. Winona Lake, IN: Brethren Evangelistic Ministries, 1989.

Jackson, Daniel J. *Manner and Content in Evangelism*. MDiv diss., Grace Theological Seminary, 1984.

James, William. *The Varieties of Religious Experience*. New York: Collier, 1970.

Johnson, Ronald W. *How Will They Hear If We Don't Listen*. Nashville: Broadman and Holman, 1994.

Kennedy, D. James. *Evangelism Explosion*. Wheaton, IL: Tyndale, 1996.

Kittel, Gerhard. "legw." In *Theological Dictionary of the New Testament*, edited and translated by Geoffrey W. Bromiley, 4:119. Grand Rapids: Eerdmans, 1973.

Klingsick, Ronald Edward. *Motivating Hesitant Witnesses to Share Their Faith through Preaching on Personal Hindrances in Evangelism*. DMin diss., Southwestern Baptist Theological Seminary, 1991.

Kostenberger, A. J. "Witness." In *Dictionary of Jesus and the Gospels*, edited by Joel B. Green et al., 1000-1004. Downers Grove, IL: InterVarsity, 1992.

Larkin, William J. "Evangelize, Evangelism." In *Evangelical Dictionary of Biblical Theology*, edited by Walter A. Elwell, 216. Grand Rapids: Baker, 1996.

Leavell, Roland Q. *The Apostle Paul: Christ's Supreme Trophy*. Grand Rapids: Baker, 1997.

Lim, D. S. "Evangelism in the Early Church." In *Dictionary of the Later New Testament and Its Developments*, edited by Ralph P. Martin and Peter H. Davids, 353-55. Downers Grove, IL: InterVarsity, 1997.

Maynard-Reid, Pedrito U. *Complete Evangelism. The Luke-Acts Model*. Scottsdale, PA: Herald, 1997.

McGavran, Donald A. *Effective Evangelism: A Theological Mandate*. Phillipsburg, NJ: Presbyterian and Reformed, 1988.

McLaren, Brian D. *The Church on the Other Side*. Grand Rapids: Zondervan, 1988.

McMillan, James H., and Sally Schumacher. *Research in Education. A Conceptual Introduction*. New York: Addison Wesley Longman, 1997.

Bibliography

Miller, Herb. *Evangelism's Open Secrets*. St. Louis: CBP, 1989.
Miller, P. D., Jr. "Syntax and Theology in Genesis XII 3a." *Vetus Testamentum* 34 (1984) 472–76.
Mitchell, Bo. *You Can't Take It with You: The Excitement of Personal Witnessing for Christ*. Nashville: Broadman, 1990.
Mouw, Richard. "Evangelism: The Very Idea." *Pro Ecclesia* 7, no. 2 (Spring 1998) 172–85.
Packer, J. I. *Evangelism and the Sovereignty of God*. Downers Grove, IL: InterVarsity, 1961.
Patton, Michael Quinn. *Qualitative Evaluation and Research Methods*. Newbury Park, CA: Sage, 1990.
Payne, Tony J., and Phillip D. Jensen. *Two Ways to Live: Know the Gospel, Share the Gospel; Participant's Manual*. Kingsford, Aus.: St. Matthias, 1989.
Petersen, Jim. *Church Without Walls*. Colorado Springs: Navpress, 1992.
———. *Evangelism as a Lifestyle*. Colorado Springs: Navpress, 1980.
———. "Proclaiming Jesus Christ as the One Universal Savior and Lord." *Evangelical Review of Theology* 20, no. 4 (1996) 385–88.
Posterski, Donald C. *Reinventing Evangelism*. Downers Grove, IL: Intervarsity, 1989.
Radmacher, Earl D. "Contemporary Evangelism Potpourri, Part One." *Bibliotheca Sacra* 123 (Jan. 1966) 40–52.
Rainer, Thomas, ed. *Evangelism in the Twenty-First Century*. Wheaton, IL: Harold Shaw, 1989.
Richardson, Rick. *Evangelism Outside the Box*. Downers Grove, IL: Intervarsity, 2000.
Rumford, Douglas J. *Soul Shaping*. Wheaton, IL: Tyndale, 1996.
Salter, Darius. *American Evangelism: Its Theology and Practice*. Grand Rapids: Baker, 1996.
Schmidt, Henry J., ed. *Witnesses of a Third Way*. Elgin, IL: Brethren, 1986.
Scobie, Geoffrey E. W. *Psychology of Religion*. New York: Wiley, 1975.
Stalker, James. *The Life of St. Paul*. New York: American Tract Society, n.d.
Stott, John R. "Christian Ministry in the Twenty-First Century, Part Two: The Church's Mission in the World." *Bibliotheca Sacra* 145 (Jul.-Sept. 1988) 243–53.
———. *The Spirit, the Church, and the World*. Downer's Grove, IL: InterVarsity, 1990.
Thiel, Larry. "Are You a Gifted Evangelist?" http://www.urbana.org/articles.cfm?RecordId+144.
Thiessen, Gerd. *Sociology of Early Palestinian Christianity*. Translated by John Bowden. Philadelphia: Fortress, 1978.
VanGemeren, Willem. *The Progress of Redemption: The Story of Salvation from Creation to the New Jerusalem*. Grand Rapids: Zondervan, 1988.
Waltke, Bruce K. and M. O'Connor. *An Introduction to Biblical Hebrew Syntax*. Winona Lake, IN: Eisenbrauns, 1990.

Bibliography

Wells, David F. *The Person of Christ: A Biblical and Historical Account of the Incarnation*. Westchester, IL: Crossway, 1984.

Weston, Paul. "Evangelism: Some Biblical and Contemporary Perspectives." *Anvil* 12, no.3 (1995) 243–53.

Wilkins, Michael J. *Following the Master: Discipleship in the Steps of Jesus*. Grand Rapids: Zondervan, 1992.

Yarchin, William. "Imperative and Promise in Genesis 12:1–3." *Studies in Biblical Theology* 10 (Oct. 1980) 164–78.

www.ingramcontent.com/pod-product-compliance
Lightning Source LLC
LaVergne TN
LVHW051709080426
835511LV00017B/2805